amazingly simple
TRIANGLE
STARS

Deceptively Easy Quilts *from* One Block

BARBARA H. CLINE

C&T PUBLISHING

Text copyright © 2015 by Barbara H. Cline

Photography and artwork copyright © 2015 by C&T Publishing, Inc.

Publisher: Amy Marson

Creative Director: Gailen Runge

Art Director/Cover Designer: Kristy Zacharias

Editor: Lynn Koolish

Technical Editor: Susan Nelsen and Mary E. Flynn

Book Designer: Kristen Yenche

Production Coordinator: Jenny Davis

Production Editor: Joanna Burgarino

Illustrator: Aliza Shalit

Photo Assistant: Mary Peyton Peppo

Instructional photography by Diane Pedersen, unless otherwise noted

Published by C&T Publishing, Inc.,
P.O. Box 1456, Lafayette, CA 94549

Attention Copy Shops: Please note the following exception—publisher and author give permission to photocopy pages 71–74.

Attention Teachers: C&T Publishing, Inc., encourages you to use this book as a text for teaching. Contact us at 800-284-1114 or ctpub.com for lesson plans and information about the C&T Creative Troupe.

We take great care to ensure that the information included in our products is accurate and presented in good faith, but no warranty is provided nor are results guaranteed. Having no control over the choices of materials or procedures used, neither the author nor C&T Publishing, Inc., shall have any liability to any person or entity with respect to any loss or damage caused directly or indirectly by the information contained in this book. For your convenience, we post an up-to-date listing of corrections on our website (ctpub.com). If a correction is not already noted, please contact our customer service department at ctinfo@ctpub.com or at P.O. Box 1456, Lafayette, CA 94549.

Trademark (™) and registered trademark (®) names are used throughout this book. Rather than use the symbols with every occurrence of a trademark or registered trademark name, we are using the names only in the editorial fashion and to the benefit of the owner, with no intention of infringement.

Library of Congress Cataloging-in-Publication Data
Cline, Barbara H.
  Amazingly simple triangle stars : deceptively easy quilts from one block / Barbara H. Cline.
      pages cm
  ISBN 978-1-60705-912-7 (soft cover)
  1. Patchwork--Patterns. 2. Quilting--Patterns. 3. Star quilts. I. Title.
  TT835.C5953 2015
  746.46--dc23
                                    2014049018

Printed in China
10 9 8 7 6 5 4 3 2 1

acknowledgments

To my husband, children, sisters, quilting friends, and students, who continue to inspire me and challenge me in my quilting arena.

To my quilting friends who wrote a life lesson for this book.

To all of the quilters in my classes, for sharing their love and joy of quilting with me.

Thank you to fabric companies Northcott and RJR Fabrics for their generosity.

And thank you to C&T Publishing—Lynn Koolish, Susan Nelsen, Roxane Cerda, Gailen Runge, Joanna Burgarino, Jenny Davis, Diane Pedersen, and Kristen Yenche.

contents

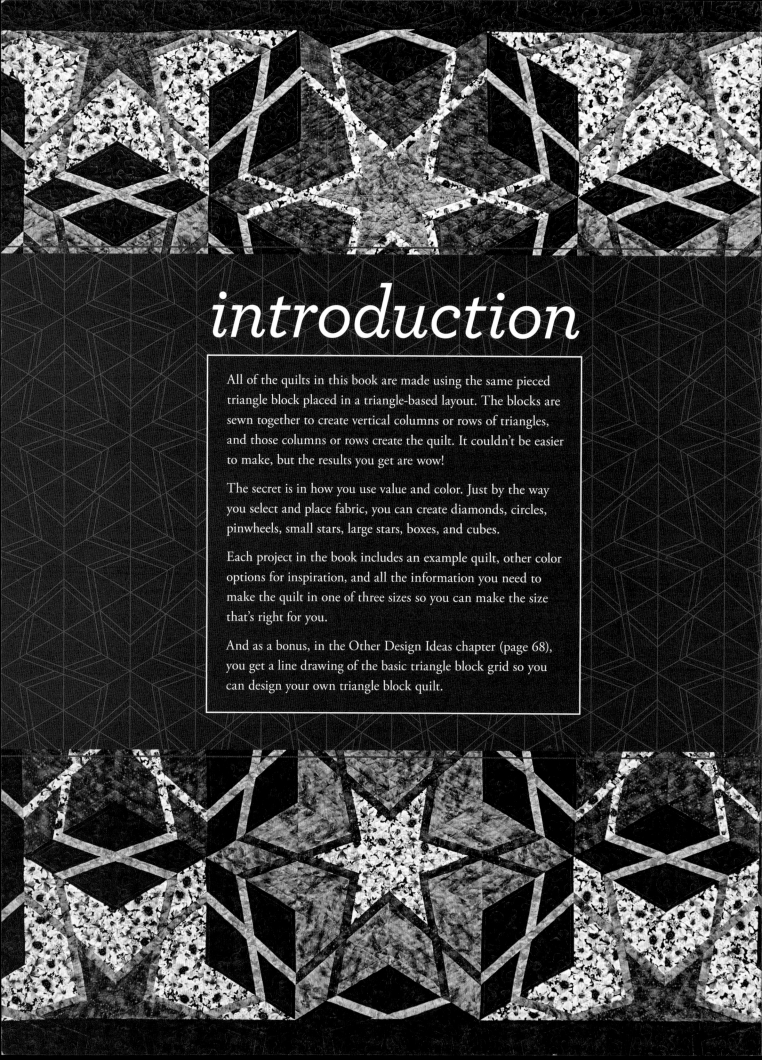

introduction

All of the quilts in this book are made using the same pieced triangle block placed in a triangle-based layout. The blocks are sewn together to create vertical columns or rows of triangles, and those columns or rows create the quilt. It couldn't be easier to make, but the results you get are wow!

The secret is in how you use value and color. Just by the way you select and place fabric, you can create diamonds, circles, pinwheels, small stars, large stars, boxes, and cubes.

Each project in the book includes an example quilt, other color options for inspiration, and all the information you need to make the quilt in one of three sizes so you can make the size that's right for you.

And as a bonus, in the Other Design Ideas chapter (page 68), you get a line drawing of the basic triangle block grid so you can design your own triangle block quilt.

triangle block BASICS

The basic triangle block is made of five different pieces and is easy to put together. Make a few practice blocks by following the instructions and these tips and tricks, and you'll be on your way in no time.

The Triangle Block

Look at the block and you will see a right and left triangle, an ice-cream cone shape, and two long slender pieces. It is very important that you lay out a complete block before you start to sew.

Notice that pieces B and C are two different shapes—piece B has a sharper point on one end, and the sharper point is always pointing down in the block.

Dr (D reversed) is on the left and D is on the right.

Pieces must be positioned like this.

The triangle block

Slender pieces (B, C)

Making Plastic Templates for the Projects

1. Make a photocopy of the Triangle block patterns (pages 72 and 73). You only need to make 5 templates: A, B, C, D/Dr, and G/Gr. (The D/Dr and G/Gr templates will be used for both pieces.)

2. Roughly cut out the shapes, leaving at least a ¼″ margin around each shape.

3. Attach the photocopy to the template plastic, using a glue stick or double-sided tape. Spread glue or place tape on the right side of the paper. Then place template plastic on top of the paper (you can see through the plastic) and cut out each template shape, just cutting off the line. Leave the paper on the template plastic so there is no need to mark the letter or grain lines on the temple plastic.

≪*making your*≫ *templates nonslip*

Add a few sandpaper dots to the paper on the underside of each template. This helps keep the templates from sliding on the fabric when you are cutting around them.

≪*tip*≫

Another easy way to make templates is to use clear self-adhesive laminate, such as Essential Self-Adhesive Laminating Sheets from C&T Publishing. After you roughly cut out the template pattern, peel off the backing from the laminating sheet, and place your templates face down on the sticky side of the laminating sheets. Then, cut out the templates as described above. Easy!

Cutting the Pieces

Using the templates to cut the pieces from fabric strips is the easiest and most efficient cutting method. It eliminates making little cuts in the fabric and requires fewer rotations of the template.

Never cut the fabric folded except where noted. The right side of the fabric always needs to be facing up. When cutting shapes from a fabric strip, rotate or slide the template into the next position; never flip the template over unless the directions specifically tell you to flip it.

CUTTING THE A SHAPE

1. Cut a strip 3¼″ × width of fabric.

2. Place the fabric strip right side up on the cutting mat and place the template on the fabric strip near an end.

3. Place the ruler on top of the template, aligning the ¼″ line of the ruler to the ¼″ line on the template, and cut with a rotary cutter. Using this method, you will never need to worry about shaving off the template plastic.

Place grain line parallel to edge of cut strip.

4. Rotate the template and continue to cut out the pieces.

Rotate template and continue cutting.

CUTTING THE B AND C SHAPES

1. Cut a strip 1¼" × width of fabric.

2. Refer to Steps 2–4 of Cutting the A Shape (page 6) to cut the B and C shapes.

CUTTING THE D AND DR TRIANGLES

1. Cut 2 strips 4¼" × width of fabric.

2. Place the strips with wrong sides together so that D and Dr triangles will be cut at the same time. You will usually need pairs of these triangles for these projects.

3. Refer to Steps 3 and 4 of Cutting the A Shape (page 6) to cut the D/Dr shapes.

CUTTING THE G AND GR TRIANGLES

1. Cut 2 strips 8¼" × width of fabric.

2. Place the strips with wrong sides together so that G and Gr triangles will be cut at the same time. You will usually need pairs of these triangles for these projects.

3. Place the template right side up on the fabric strip near an end, aligning the bottom edge of the template with the strip edge.

4. Refer to Steps 3 and 4 of Cutting the A Shape (page 6) to cut the G/Gr shapes.

«tip»

When cutting the pieces for each project, stack, label, and keep each shape together. Because D/Dr and G/Gr pieces are cut together, separate them and label each stack so you don't get them mixed up.

Cutting Chart

This cutting chart shows how many pieces can be cut from a strip of fabric and the width of strip that needs to be cut for the specified template. Strips are based on 40″-wide fabric.

TEMPLATE	WIDTH OF STRIPS	1 STRIP	2 STRIPS	3 STRIPS	4 STRIPS	5 STRIPS	6 STRIPS	7 STRIPS	8 STRIPS
A	3¼"	8	16	24	32	40	48	56	64
B	1¼"	6	12	18	24	30	36	42	48
C	1¼"	6	12	18	24	30	36	42	48
D*	4¼"	11	22	33	44	55	66	77	88
Dr*	4¼"	11	22	33	44	55	66	77	88

* D and Dr can be cut in pairs by placing 2 strips wrong sides together and then cutting with the D template. This will cut pairs of D/Dr.

Making the Triangle Block

All seam allowances are ¼".

1. Arrange pieces A, B, C, D, and Dr for the block as shown.

Pieces arranged in correct orientation

2. With right sides together, sew B to A. Notice the position of B on A—the stitching line falls in the V space at the top and bottom. Press toward the darker fabric.

Sew B to A.

3. With right sides together, place C on top of the A/B unit. Begin stitching at the V to sew the pieces together. Press toward the darker fabric.

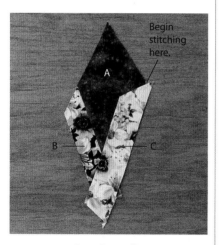

Sew C to A/B.

4. With right sides together, place D on top of the A/B/C unit and sew them together. Press toward the darker fabric.

Sew D to A/B/C.

5. With right sides together, place Dr on top of the A/B/C/D unit. Press toward the darker fabric.

Sew Dr to A/B/C/D.

6. Trim off any pieces of fabric that extend beyond the triangle.

A Few Important Things to Know

BIAS EDGES

The triangle block used for the quilts in the book has two bias sides, which can easily stretch out of shape and become distorted. I recommend a light spray starch alternative (such as Mary Ellen's Best Press) on all fabrics to help keep them from stretching. I spray and iron the whole piece of fabric before I begin cutting. Always be aware that fabrics can stretch, so be gentle as you handle fabrics and try to keep them from stretching.

Basic Supplies

✪ Rotary cutter

✪ Rotary cutting mat

✪ Rotary/acrylic cutting rulers. I recommend 4″ × 14″ (good to use when cutting strips into pieces), 6″ × 24″ (good for cutting yardage into strips), and 15″ × 15″.

✪ Pins

✪ Chalk pencil, roller, or removable marker for marking fabric

✪ Sewing thread

✪ ¼″ presser foot for your sewing machine

✪ Scissors for clipping threads and trimming dog-ears

✪ Seam ripper

✪ Template plastic

✪ Sandpaper dots

✪ Glue stick

✪ Double-sided tape

✪ Iron and ironing board

✪ Mary Ellen's Best Press spray starch alternative

Using a Design Wall

If you don't currently have a design wall, I urge you to get or make one, even if it's a piece of flannel or batting that you temporarily put up or a few sheets of insulation or foam core board that you store under the bed when they aren't being used. For all of the quilts in this book, you'll be arranging all the elements before sewing them together.

PROJECTS

Large Diamonds Runner

The Elegance of Overlapping Diamonds

FINISHED SIZE: 18″ × 62″

Project Lesson:
A Smaller Project to Get Started

This is a great project to get you started on making Triangle Star quilts. Its smaller size allows you to master the technique quickly and you can move on to making the larger quilts in this book.

When you look at this table runner your eyes see the stars on top the diamonds and the diamonds are overlapping each other. Study this quilt and you can see the diamonds in this project are larger diamonds than *Shenandoah Heartland* (page 14).

Materials

	TABLE RUNNER **18″ × 62″**
Print	½ yard
Navy	¾ yard
Turquoise	½ yard
Gray	1 yard
Binding	½ yard
Backing	1⅓ yards
Batting	24″ × 68″

Cutting

Refer to Triangle Block Basics (page 5) as needed to cut strips for A, B, C, and D/Dr. Use patterns A, B, C, D/Dr, G/Gr, and H (pages 72–74) to make templates. Label each stack of cut pieces.

	TABLE RUNNER **18″ × 62″**
Print	
Template A	18
Navy	
Template D/Dr	10 pairs
9″ × WOF	1 strip; subcut template H
Template H	2
Turquoise	
Template D/Dr	8 pairs
Gray	
Template B	18
Template C	18
9″ × WOF	2 strips; subcut templates G/Gr and H
Template G/Gr	8 pairs
Template H	4
Binding	
2¼″ × WOF	5 strips

Make the Triangle Blocks

All seam allowances are ¼". Refer to Making the Triangle Block (page 7) as needed.

1. Sew a gray B and gray C to all the A pieces to make the star blades. Press the seams toward A.

Make 18.

2. To complete each triangle block, add matching D and Dr pieces to each A/B/C unit. Press the seams toward D/Dr.

Make 10.

Make 8.

Assemble the Quilt

1. Arrange the triangle blocks and background pieces as shown in the quilt assembly diagram (below).

2. Sew the triangles into vertical columns. Press the seams open.

3. Sew the columns together. Press the seams open.

Quilt assembly

Finish the Quilt

Refer to Quiltmaking Basics (page 75) to layer, quilt, and bind your quilt. Quilt as desired. Use the 2¼" binding strips to finish the quilt.

Detail of quilting: Straight lines help define each diamond.

Color Options

Yellow accent fabric is placed down center. Now there are just small diamonds.

Red, white, and blue fabric colors create this wonderful July 4th party table runner. Using stripe fabrics in stars makes them spin.

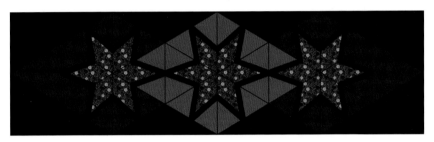

Christmas colors make nice star table runners.

Life Lesson:
Mother Knows Best

I come from a family of seven girls. When we were young, our mother made all of our clothes. Once we reached middle school, it was our responsibility to make our own clothes. This meant a lot of sewing was done in our home. At first, making garments was not something I enjoyed; but with practice, time, and patience, I soon started to enjoy sewing.

Mother had a rule for us girls, and that rule was that we could not start a new project until the previous project was finished. I remember thinking on different occasions how I wanted to buy fabric for a new project, but I was still in the process of working on another one. This was a great incentive for me to finish my garment, quilt, or craft project.

Years later when I started making many quilts, I would start a quilt and before I was done I would let my wants get the best of me and I would start another one. Soon I realized my quilt project stack was getting out of control. I remembered the rule Mother had made at home and decided that it would be a good rule for me to follow in my quiltmaking. I made the decision to finish all the projects I had started before beginning on any others. This took a few months to tackle, but when I was done I had such a feeling of accomplishment. I now have only three projects on the go at one time. One is a machine project, one is an appliqué project, and one is a hand-stitched velvet comforter. It is not only a great incentive to keep me quilting, but it also means I always look forward to my next new project.

—Barbara H. Cline

Shenandoah Heartland

FINISHED SIZE: 62″ × 72″ (throw size)

Project Lesson:
Blend from One Color of Fabric to Another

The design of this quilt features stars outlined with white—the star is the same color as the background fabric in each diamond and the fabrics blend from color to color diagonally across the quilt.

For this quilt, you will need twenty fabrics in colors and values that blend from color to color.

When picking fabrics, I recommend starting with three to five basic colors that you want to use and then finding the values that allow you to move from color to color. You may have four values of one color while having more or fewer values of another color. Whatever number of color values you have, the values should flow from color to color.

For example, starting with blue, yellow, and green:

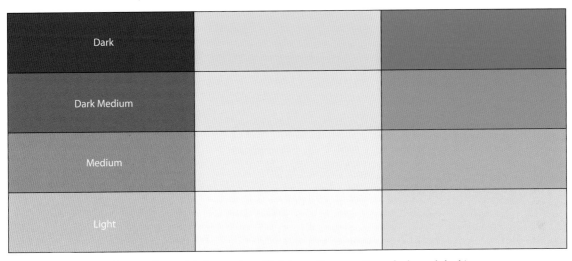

Three colors with four values (light, medium, medium-dark, and dark)

When blending from one color to another either the lightest or the darkest values should be next to each other, as shown.

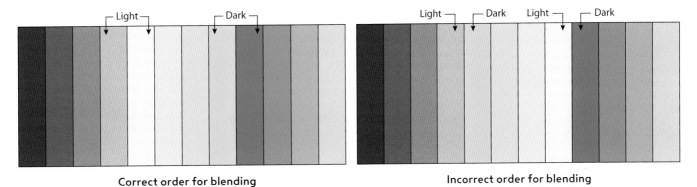

Correct order for blending   **Incorrect order for blending**

For the outline of the stars, choose a fabric that will contrast with *all* of the other fabrics. Notice how you lose the gray when it is over the light blue. The best outline colors in this example are white and black.

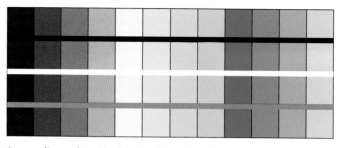

Auditioning outline color: black and white show best contrast on these samples.

Materials

Choose 20 fabrics that blend as described in the project lesson (page 15). Align the fabrics to flow in value from color to color, and number them 1–20. Using this chart, you can determine the amount for each fabric.

	THROW 62″ × 72″	TWIN 70″ × 90″	QUEEN 93″ × 108″
Fabric 1	¼ yard	¼ yard	⅝ yard
Fabric 2	⅓ yard	⅓ yard	⅝ yard
Fabric 3	½ yard	½ yard	⅞ yard
Fabric 4	½ yard	½ yard	⅞ yard
Fabric 5	½ yard	⅝ yard	1 yard
Fabric 6	½ yard	½ yard	⅝ yard
Fabric 7	⅝ yard	⅝ yard	⅝ yard
Fabric 8	⅝ yard	⅝ yard	⅞ yard
Fabric 9	⅞ yard	⅞ yard	⅞ yard
Fabric 10	⅞ yard	⅞ yard	1 yard
Fabric 11	⅞ yard	⅞ yard	⅞ yard
Fabric 12	⅞ yard	⅞ yard	⅞ yard
Fabric 13	⅝ yard	⅞ yard	⅞ yard
Fabric 14	⅝ yard	⅞ yard	⅞ yard
Fabric 15	½ yard	⅞ yard	⅞ yard
Fabric 16	½ yard	⅝ yard	⅞ yard
Fabric 17	½ yard	⅝ yard	⅞ yard
Fabric 18	½ yard	½ yard	⅞ yard
Fabric 19	¼ yard	½ yard	⅞ yard
Fabric 20	¼ yard	½ yard	⅞ yard
White	2 yards	2½ yards	3¾ yards
Binding	⅝ yard	¾ yard	⅞ yard
Backing	4½ yards	5½ yards	9⅓ yards
Batting	70″ × 80″	78″ × 98″	111″ × 116″

Cutting

Refer to Triangle Block Basics (page 5) as needed to make templates and cut strips. Use patterns A, B, C, D, and Dr (pages 72 and 73). Label each stack of cut pieces. This chart also indicates how many blocks to make from each fabric.

	THROW	TWIN	QUEEN		THROW	TWIN	QUEEN
Fabric 1	Make 1 block.	Make 1 block.	Make 9 blocks.	**Fabric 12**	Make 12 blocks.	Make 14 blocks.	Make 16 blocks.
Template A	1	1	9	Template A	12	14	16
Template D/Dr	1 pair	1 pair	9 pairs	Template D/Dr	12 pairs	14 pairs	16 pairs
Fabric 2	Make 2 blocks.	Make 2 blocks.	Make 11 blocks.	**Fabric 13**	Make 11 blocks.	Make 14 blocks.	Make 17 blocks.
Template A	2	2	11	Template A	11	14	17
Template D/Dr	2 pairs	2 pairs	11 pairs	Template D/Dr	11 pairs	14 pairs	17 pairs
Fabric 3	Make 4 blocks.	Make 6 blocks.	Make 14 blocks.	**Fabric 14**	Make 10 blocks.	Make 14 blocks.	Make 16 blocks.
Template A	4	6	14	Template A	10	14	16
Template D/Dr	4 pairs	6 pairs	14 pairs	Template D/Dr	10 pairs	14 pairs	16 pairs
Fabric 4	Make 5 blocks.	Make 8 blocks.	Make 17 blocks.	**Fabric 15**	Make 8 blocks.	Make 12 blocks.	Make 17 blocks.
Template A	5	8	17	Template A	8	12	17
Template D/Dr	5 pairs	8 pairs	17 pairs	Template D/Dr	8 pairs	12 pairs	17 pairs
Fabric 5	Make 6 blocks.	Make 10 blocks.	Make 19 blocks.	**Fabric 16**	Make 7 blocks.	Make 11 blocks.	Make 17 blocks.
Template A	6	10	19	Template A	7	11	17
Template D/Dr	6 pairs	10 pairs	19 pairs	Template D/Dr	7 pairs	11 pairs	17 pairs
Fabric 6	Make 8 blocks.	Make 8 blocks.	Make 9 blocks.	**Fabric 17**	Make 6 blocks.	Make 10 blocks.	Make 16 blocks.
Template A	8	8	9	Template A	6	10	16
Template D/Dr	8 pairs	8 pairs	9 pairs	Template D/Dr	6 pairs	10 pairs	16 pairs
Fabric 7	Make 9 blocks.	Make 9 blocks.	Make 11 blocks.	**Fabric 18**	Make 4 blocks.	Make 8 blocks.	Make 17 blocks.
Template A	9	9	11	Template A	4	8	17
Template D/Dr	9 pairs	9 pairs	11 pairs	Template D/Dr	4 pairs	8 pairs	17 pairs
Fabric 8	Make 10 blocks.	Make 10 blocks.	Make 14 blocks.	**Fabric 19**	Make 3 blocks.	Make 7 blocks.	Make 16 blocks.
Template A	10	10	14	Template A	3	7	16
Template D/Dr	10 pairs	10 pairs	14 pairs	Template D/Dr	3 pairs	7 pairs	16 pairs
Fabric 9	Make 12 blocks.	Make 12 blocks.	Make 17 blocks.	**Fabric 20**	Make 2 blocks.	Make 6 blocks.	Make 14 blocks.
Template A	12	12	17	Template A	2	6	14
Template D/Dr	12 pairs	12 pairs	17 pairs	Template D/Dr	2 pairs	6 pairs	14 pairs
Fabric 10	Make 12 blocks.	Make 13 blocks.	Make 19 blocks.	**White**			
Template A	12	13	19	Template B	144	189	300
Template D/Dr	12 pairs	13 pairs	19 pairs	Template C	144	189	300
Fabric 11	Make 12 blocks.	Make 14 blocks.	Make 14 blocks.	**Binding** (2¼" × **WOF***)	7 strips	9 strips	11 strips
Template A	12	14	14				
Template D/Dr	12 pairs	14 pairs	14 pairs				

* WOF = width of fabric

Make the Triangle Blocks

All seam allowances are ¼".

1. Refer to Making the Triangle Block (page 7). Arrange a block with matching color A, D, and Dr pieces with white B and C pieces. Sew the block together and trim off any pieces that extend beyond the triangle block.

2. Refer to the cutting chart (page 17) for the total number of blocks from each fabric. Label each block with the fabric number.

Assemble the Quilt

1. Refer to the quilt assembly diagram (pages 18 and 19) for your size quilt. Arrange the triangle blocks as shown.

2. Sew the triangle blocks into vertical columns. Press the seams open.

3. Sew the columns together. Press the seams open.

4. Trim off the triangle blocks as needed to make the quilt even on the top and bottom edges.

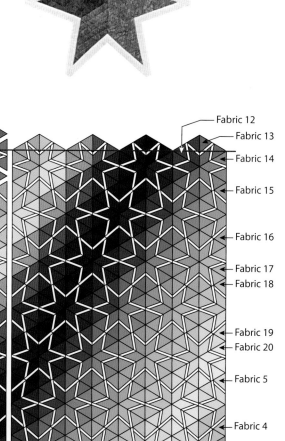

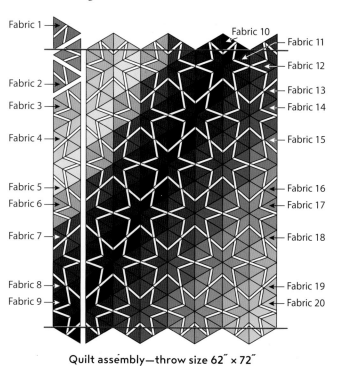

Quilt assembly—throw size 62˝ × 72˝

Quilt assembly—twin size 70˝ × 80˝

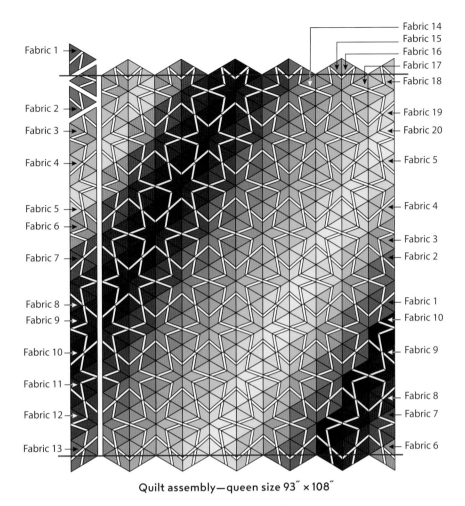

Fabric 1
Fabric 2
Fabric 3
Fabric 4
Fabric 5
Fabric 6
Fabric 7
Fabric 8
Fabric 9
Fabric 10
Fabric 11
Fabric 12
Fabric 13

Fabric 14
Fabric 15
Fabric 16
Fabric 17
Fabric 18
Fabric 19
Fabric 20
Fabric 5
Fabric 4
Fabric 3
Fabric 2
Fabric 1
Fabric 10
Fabric 9
Fabric 8
Fabric 7
Fabric 6

Quilt assembly—queen size 93˝ × 108˝

Finish the Quilt

Refer to Quiltmaking Basics (page 75) to layer, quilt, and bind the quilt. Quilt as desired. Use the 2¼˝-wide binding strips to finish the quilt.

Detail of quilting: Notice how quilting changes direction.

Color Options

Blending colors with dark outline

Many colors in one quilt (no blending)

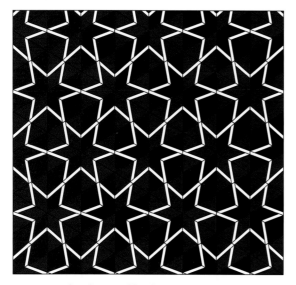

Two-color diamond background (no blending)

Two-color background with multicolored stars
and solid-color stars (no blending)

My love of sewing began at a very early age. My mother was my teacher. She made all my clothes and I loved all of them. They were so beautiful. She would give me the leftover fabric scraps and I'd make doll clothes. Hours were spent by her side learning the art of sewing.

My first sewing machine was a graduation gift from my mom and dad. I remember how excited I was. It had fifteen built-in stitches. That machine went with me all over the country. It was the machine I learned to quilt with. The lady at my local quilt shop in Texas said all I needed was a machine with a straight stitch. I signed up for a class and then another and yet another one after that. I was hooked.

The wonderful thing about a quilting class is the way it draws people together, creating friendships and bonds that continue long after the class ends. Quilting classes became an avenue for me to connect with folks—my husband and I moved so often because of his job. I have quilting buddies all over this country and the quilts I made side-by-side with them are a visible sign of times spent together.

For the last seven years, quilting has been a way for me to rekindle that sewing connection with my mom. She lives in Virginia and I live in Georgia. Every month I go to Virginia and we take a quilting class together. We've made many quilts, but the part I treasure most is the time I get to spend with my mom.

—Twilla Dove

Autumn's Path of Stone

FINISHED SIZE: 86˝ × 107˝ (queen size)

Project Lesson:
Change Star Colors and Background Colors to Create a Completely Different Quilt

What makes this quilt so different from *Shenandoah Heartland* (page 14)? The first difference is that the color inside the stars is different from the background color. The second difference is that the background fabric forms circles instead of diamonds. This quilt uses four groups of colors: blue, gray, green, and brown. The stars inside the circles are a lighter value of the circle fabrics, the stars circling each circle are a light cream printed fabric, and the fabric outlining the stars is black to make the stars stand out even more.

Materials

	WALL 45" × 47"	DOUBLE 78" × 90"	QUEEN 86" × 107"
Black	⅞ yard	2¾ yards	3 yards
Cream	¾ yard	1⅞ yards	2⅜ yards
Light blue I	¼ yard	¼ yard	¼ yard
Blue II	¼ yard	¼ yard	¼ yard
Blue III	½ yard	¾ yard	¾ yard
Blue IV	½ yard	¾ yard	¾ yard
Blue V	-	¾ yard	¾ yard
Light gray I	¼ yard	¼ yard	¼ yard
Gray II	¼ yard	¼ yard	¼ yard
Gray III	½ yard	⅞ yard	⅞ yard
Gray IV	½ yard	¾ yard	¾ yard
Gray V	½ yard	¾ yard	¾ yard
Light green I	¼ yard	¼ yard	¼ yard
Green II	-	¼ yard	¼ yard
Green III	¾ yard	¾ yard	¾ yard
Green IV	-	¾ yard	¾ yard
Green V	-	⅝ yard	¾ yard
Light brown I	¼ yard	¼ yard	¼ yard
Brown II	¼ yard	¼ yard	¼ yard
Brown III	-	¼ yard	¼ yard
Brown IV	-	½ yard	¾ yard
Brown V	-	¾ yard	¾ yard
Brown VI	½ yard	¾ yard	⅞ yard
Binding	½ yard	¾ yard	⅞ yard
Backing	3 yards	7½ yards	7⅞ yards
Batting	53" × 55"	86" × 96"	94" × 115"

Cutting

Refer to Triangle Block Basics (page 5) as needed. Use patterns A, B, C, D, and Dr (pages 72 and 73) to make templates. Number fabric colors from lightest to darkest. Label each stack of cut pieces.

Black			
Template B	66	210	230
Template C	66	210	230
Border (4½″ × WOF*)	-	-	10 strips
Cream			
Template A	48	150	170
Light blue I			
Template A	3	6	6
Blue II			
Template A	3	6	6
Blue III			
Template A	-	6	6
Template D/Dr	8 pairs	20 pairs	21 pairs
Template D	1	-	-
Template Dr	-	1	-
Blue IV			
Template D/Dr	8 pairs	18 pairs	18 pairs
Template D	1	-	-
Blue V			
Template D/Dr	-	20 pairs	21 pairs
Template D	-	1	-
Light gray I			
Template A	2	6	6
Light gray II			
Template A	2	6	6
Gray III			
Template D/Dr	7 pairs	23 pairs	24 pairs
Template D	-	1	-
Gray IV			
Template D/Dr	7 pairs	14 pairs	17 pairs

Gray V			
Template D/Dr	8 pairs	18 pairs	18 pairs
Template Dr	1	-	-
Light green I			
Template A	6	6	6
Green II			
Template A	-	6	6
Green III			
Template D/Dr	18 pairs	18 pairs	18 pairs
Green IV			
Template D/Dr	-	14 pairs	17 pairs
Green V			
Template D/Dr	-	10 pairs	13 pairs
Light brown I			
Template A	3	6	6
Brown II			
Template A	3	6	6
Brown III			
Template A	-	6	6
Brown IV			
Template D/Dr	-	11 pairs	17 pairs
Brown V			
Template D/Dr	-	20 pairs	21 pairs
Template Dr	-	1	-
Brown VI			
Template D/Dr	8 pairs	22 pairs	25 pairs
Template Dr	1	-	-
Binding (2¼″ × WOF*)	5 strips	9 strips	10 strips

* WOF = width of fabric

Make the Triangle Blocks

All seam allowances are ¼″. Refer to Making the Triangle Block (page 7) as needed.

Sew a black B and a black C piece onto all the A pieces. Make 66 units for the wall size, 210 units for the double, and 230 for the queen. Press the seams toward the black.

Make all units.

Assemble the Quilt

1. Find your quilt size within this diagram to arrange the A/B/C units into stars on a design wall.

2. Place 6 matching D and 6 matching Dr pieces around a star center to make a hexagon.

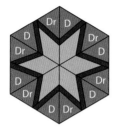

Make hexagon.

3. Place 12 more matching D and 12 more matching Dr pieces around the hexagon from Step 2 as shown.

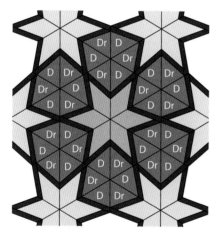

Pieces form a circle.

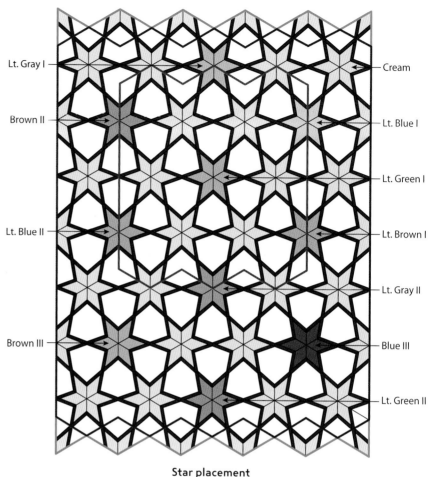

Star placement

4. Repeat Steps 3 and 4 for each color of circle.

«*alert!*»

It is easy to place a D or Dr in the wrong spot. First add the D and Dr on both sides of the A/B/C unit around the colored center star, and then add the other D and Dr triangles to complete the circle.

---

5. When all pieces are placed in position, sew the Dr to B and the D to C, completing each triangle block. Press the seams toward the black. Replace the blocks on the design wall.

6. Refer to the quilt assembly diagrams (page 25). Sew the triangles into columns. Press the seams open.

7. Sew the columns together. Press the seams open.

8. Trim the triangle blocks as needed at the top and bottom to make the quilt even on the edges as shown in the quilt assembly diagrams (page 25).

9. Refer to Borders (page 76) to add the black 4½" border strips to the queen-size quilt.

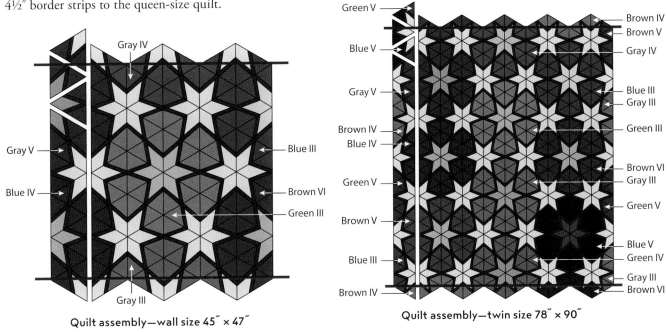

Quilt assembly—wall size 45˝ × 47˝

Quilt assembly—twin size 78˝ × 90˝

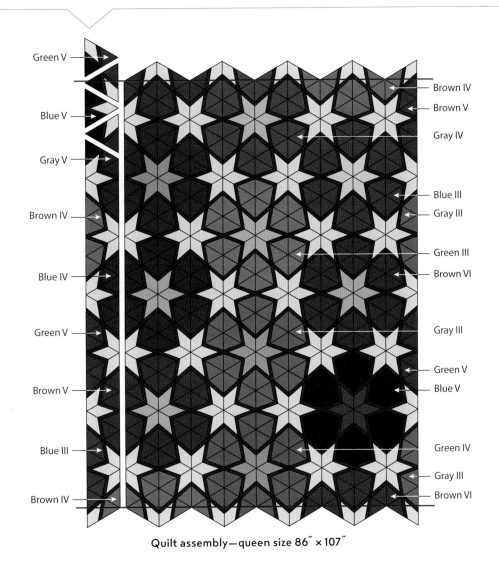

Quilt assembly—queen size 86˝ × 107˝

Finish the Quilt

Refer to Quiltmaking Basics (page 75) to layer, quilt, and bind the quilt. Quilt as desired. Use the 2¼″ binding strips to finish the quilt.

Detail of quilting: Circles quilted within circle emphasize circles; echo quilting inside of stars.

Color Options

Color placement creates one large circle.

Color placement creates one large faceted circle with faceted stars.

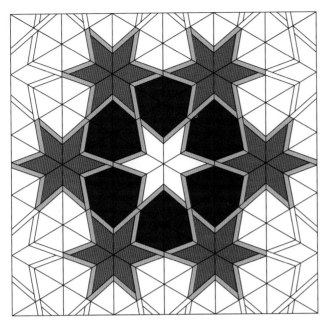

Color placement creates one large circle
with center star matching background.

Bright color option with alternate circle focus

Grandmother Good was a diminutive lady around five feet tall, but she stands out as a giant example of true beauty. She was born into a large family in the late nineteenth century, but she didn't let the hard things in life smother out the beautiful ones. With only an elementary school education, she was well versed in and wrote exquisite poetry. She knew how to use simple flowers, roses, and trees to create beauty around the home, but her special gift was creating lovely quilts.

Grandmother gave me a piece of fabric in yellow to brown hues when I was a young girl. Thus began my journey into quiltmaking. I chose the Dahlia pattern for my first project and painstakingly attempted to create a quilt. After the top was together, I was invited to Grandmother's house to learn the art of hand quilting. Day after day, she patiently taught me how to get the first stitch on the needle and make those tiny stitches. But we did more than quilt at Grandmother's house. We ate tasty home-cooked meals, sang, read scripture, had deep discussions, and looked out over the valley from the picture window. As we savored the simple, good things in life, a desire was kindled in my heart for genuine inner beauty.

My first quilt isn't all that impressive now, but it's priceless to me because it's a reminder of the lesson I learned from my dear grandmother about what is truly beautiful.

—Joyce Horst

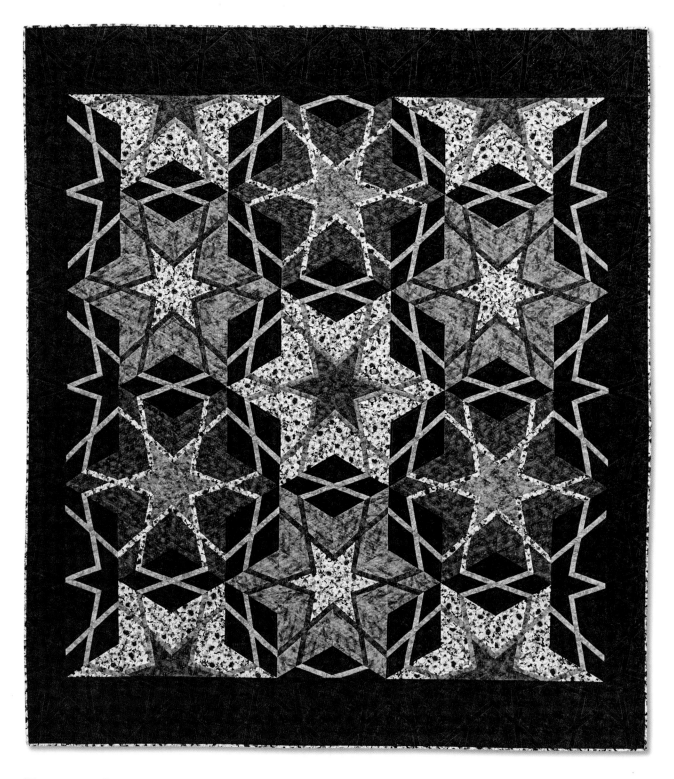

Evening Primrose

FINISHED SIZE: 90˝ × 100˝ (queen size)

Project Lesson:
Make a Star Inside a Star

The large stars that are purple, blue, and print echo the small stars, creating a star inside a star. The black diamonds around the large stars enhance each large star with contrast while the light blue X in the black diamond provides movement around the stars. Where did the rest of the small stars go? Look where the three large star tips come together and there is a small star. Because the small stars are part of the large stars and part of the black diamond, they are lost until you study the quilt and find them.

Materials

	WALL 31" × 36"	DOUBLE 78" × 81"	QUEEN 90" × 100"
Purple	¼ yard	2¼ yards	2¼ yards
Print	¾ yard	2¼ yards	2¼ yards
Blue	¼ yard	2¼ yards	2¼ yards
Light blue	¼ yard	1⅛ yards	1⅛ yards
Black	¾ yard	3 yards	3 yards
Border	-	-	2⅝ yards
Binding	⅜ yard	¾ yard	⅞ yard
Batting	39" × 44"	86" × 89"	98" × 108"
Backing	1¼ yards	7¼ yards	8¼ yards

Cutting

Refer to Triangle Block Basics (page 5) as needed to make templates and cut strips. Use patterns A, B, C, D, and Dr (pages 72 and 73). Label each stack of cut pieces.

	WALL	DOUBLE	QUEEN
Purple			
Template A	-	36	36
Template B	12	44	44
Template C	12	44	44
Template D/Dr	-	36 pairs	36 pairs
Print			
Template A	6	40	40
Template B	-	36	36
Template C	-	36	36
Template D/Dr	12 pairs	44 pairs	44 pairs
Blue			
Template A	6	40	40
Template B	-	36	36
Template C	-	36	36
Template D/Dr	-	36 pairs	36 pairs
Light blue			
Template B	12	74	74
Template C	12	74	74
Black			
Template A	12	74	74
Template D/Dr	12 pairs	74 pairs	74 pairs
Border			
10" × LOF*	-	-	2 strips
6½" × LOF*	-	-	2 strips
Binding (2¼" × WOF)**	4 strips	9 strips	10 strips

* LOF = length of fabric

** WOF = width of fabric

Make the Triangle Blocks

All seam allowances are ¼". Refer to Making the Triangle Block (page 7) as needed.

Make the following triangle blocks as shown.

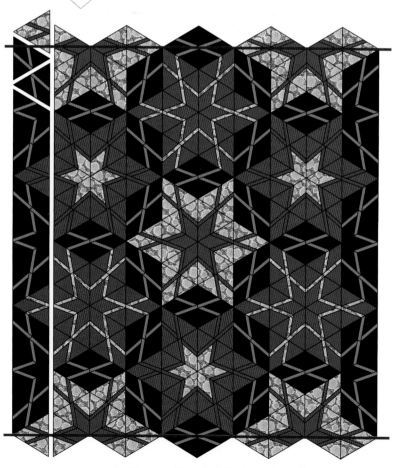

Wall	6	6	-	-
Double	22	22	18	18
Queen	22	22	18	18

Wall		-	12
Double	18	18	74
Queen	18	18	74

Quilt assembly—double size 78˝ × 81˝

Assemble the Quilt

1. Arrange the triangle blocks as shown in the quilt assembly diagrams (pages 30 and 31).

2. Sew the triangles into vertical columns. Press the seams open.

3. Sew the columns together. Press the seams open.

4. Trim off the triangle blocks at the top and bottom of the quilt as needed on the twin size and queen size.

5. For the queen-size quilt only, refer to Borders (page 76) to use the border 6½˝ strips for side borders and the border 10˝ strips for the top and bottom borders.

Quilt assembly—wall size 31˝ × 36˝

Quilt assembly—queen size 90˝ × 100˝

Finish the Quilt

Refer to Quiltmaking Basics (page 75) to layer, quilt, and bind the quilt. Quilt as desired. Use the 2¼˝ binding strips to finish the quilt.

Detail of quilting: Straight lines emphasize larger stars while feathers are featured in smaller stars.

Color Options

The white fabric around the bright-colored stars creates a solid-looking background and really makes the stars stand out.

This color combination draws your eyes to both the small stars and the large stars.

This scrappy brown version makes the lattice stand out, moving your eyes around the quilt as well as emphasizing the hexagon shapes around the stars.

This color option has six large white stars around one large blue star. The thin strips in the brown diamonds are also brown, enhancing the large stars. The brown provides contrast to make the stars really pop.

When I was young, we sewed all of our own dresses. My older sister and my mom taught me how to sew. We ironed every seam after we had sewn it to make sure everything fit well and was nice and neat. One thing we never did was wash our fabric before using it. We didn't pay any attention to the type of fabric it was; if we liked it, we bought it.

One day we found this beautiful fabric so we bought it, brought it home, cut it out, and carefully sewed it together, making sure we had everything just perfect. Oh, it fit so beautifully and I absolutely loved it. I wore it one time and then washed it. Alas! It shrank to about half its size. I just felt sick. I had put all that careful work into making it and only got to wear it once.

This was a sad lesson, and one I never forgot, but we learned to look at the content of the fabric and whether or not it was washable.

Just as you should always remember to check the content of any fabric you buy, the same way in life you should pay attention to things that seem unimportant, or too small to matter. Every little thing is important!

—Linda Tice

Windmill Storm

FINISHED SIZE: 51″ × 65″ (wall size)

Project Lesson:
Choose and Use Fabrics with Three Values

As you study this quilt, you can see three pinwheels touch each other in two places. When choosing the fabrics for this quilt, you need to use three different values each time three pinwheels touch each other.

	Blues	Browns	Grays
Dark values			
Medium values			
Light values			

Three colors in three values

Look at the example below. There are three dark fabrics in the first block. Squint your eyes and they disappear into one piece of fabric. The second block has two dark values with one medium blue fabric. Squint your eyes and you can see the blue fabric is more noticeable and the other two blend together. On the third block squint again and now you see all three fabrics. This is a great way to test fabrics before you buy. Get six feet away, squint your eyes, and make sure you see three distinct pieces of each colorway. Here are three random colors I have chosen for an example. Hold the book six feet away and squint your eyes.

Block 1—Shapes are all same value so viewer sees only whole square.

Block 2—Brown and gray are both dark and show as one piece.

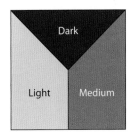

Block 3—With three distinct values, you see all three shapes.

Materials

	WALL 51" × 65"	THROW 54" × 78"	QUEEN 95" × 107"
Navy I (dark)	½ yard	1 yard	1 yard
Rust (light)	½ yard	1 yard	1½ yards
Gray print (medium)	½ yard	⅞ yard	1¾ yards
Tan (light)	½ yard	1 yard	1½ yards
Navy II (dark)	½ yard	-	1 yard
Background	2¼ yards	2⅝ yards	4 yards
Light blue	1¼ yards	1¾ yards	2¾ yards
Inside border	¼ yard	-	¾ yard
Border	-	-	2 yards
Binding	½ yard	⅝ yard	⅞ yard
Backing	3⅜ yards	4⅞ yards	8⅝ yards
Batting	59" × 73"	62" × 86"	103" × 115"

Cutting

Refer to Triangle Block Basics (page 5) as needed to make templates and cut strips. Use patterns A, B, C, D, and Dr (pages 72 and 73). Label each stack of cut pieces.

	WALL	THROW	QUEEN
Navy I			
Template A	6	18	18
Template D/Dr	6 pairs	18 pairs	18 pairs
Rust			
Template A	6	18	30
Template D/Dr	6 pairs	18 pairs	30 pairs
Gray print			
Template A	6	12	36
Template D/Dr	6 pairs	12 pairs	36 pairs
Tan			
Template A	6	18	30
Template D/Dr	6 pairs	18 pairs	30 pairs
Navy II			
Template A	6	-	18
Template D/Dr	6 pairs	-	18 pairs

	WALL	THROW	QUEEN
Background			
Template A	48	64	96
Template D/Dr	48 pairs	64 pairs	96 pairs
Light blue			
Template B	78	130	228
Template C	78	130	228
Inside border			
1½" × WOF*	5 strips	-	-
2½" × WOF*	-	-	9 strips
Border			
3½" × WOF*	6 strips	-	-
5½" × WOF*	-	-	10 strips
Binding			
2¼" × WOF*	6 strips	9 strips	11 strips

WOF = width of fabric

Make the Pinwheels

All seam allowances are ¼". Refer to Making the Triangle Block (page 7) as needed.

1. Sew a light blue B and light blue C to all the A pieces to make the star blades. Press the seams toward the light blue.

Use all A pieces.

2. Arrange the A/B/C units on a design wall, creating stars as shown in this example of the wall size. Refer to the quilt assembly diagrams (pages 37 and 38) for the other quilt sizes. Six of the star blades make a star.

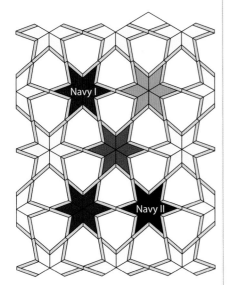

Place each color of star and the background stars.

3. Place 6 navy I Dr pieces around the navy I star as shown. Then add 6 navy I D pieces to the tips of the Dr pieces, creating a pinwheel, as shown.

4. Repeat Step 3 with matching pieces for each pinwheel.

5. Place all background D and Dr pieces according to the quilt assembly diagrams (pages 37 and 38).

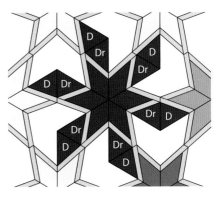

Make navy pinwheel.

6. Block by block, sew the D and Dr pieces to the star tips. Trim off any pieces that extend beyond the units. Return the blocks to the design wall.

Assemble the Quilt

1. Sew the triangle blocks into vertical columns for the wall size and horizontal rows for the throw and queen sizes. Press the seams open.

2. Sew the columns/rows together. Press the seams open. Trim the sides of the quilt as shown in the quilt assembly diagrams.

3. Refer to Borders (page 76). Use the 1½" strips for the inner border and the 3½" strips for the outer border on the wall size. Use the 2½" strips for the inner border and the 5½" strips for the outer border for the queen size. (No border is provided for the throw size.)

Quilt assembly—wall size 51˝ × 65˝

Quilt assembly—throw size 54″ × 78″

Quilt assembly—queen size 95″ × 107″

Finish the Quilt

Refer to Quiltmaking Basics (page 75) to layer, quilt, and bind the quilt. Quilt as desired. Use the 2¼″ binding strips to finish the quilt.

Detail of quilting: Parallel lines in pinwheels emphasize linear nature of shapes, and decorative filler in background helps set pinwheels apart.

Color Options

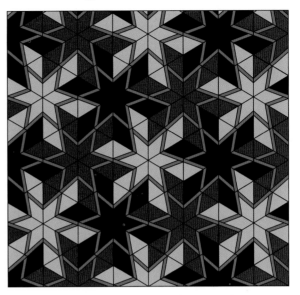

The brilliant bright green outline provides nice contrast with the three pinwheel colors.

Black, white, and gray emphasize the value differences. The fuchsia outlines look as though they are on a different plane.

The outlines around the stars are all the same as the yellow stars, giving the quilt a different look. The black and the yellow provide a bright contrast.

Monochromatic color scheme—it's all in the values.

Coming Together

FINISHED SIZE: 67″ × 77″ (throw size)

Project Lesson:
Stack the Fabrics to Create a Design Inside the Stars

The stars are placed randomly throughout this quilt. They are created by fussy cutting the fabric into strips and then using layered cutting (page 46) to cut the points of the stars from the strips. When using this cutting method, you are always in for a good surprise at the designs created in the different stars.

Materials

	WALL 51″ × 50″	THROW 67″ × 77″	QUEEN 90″ × 104″
Large print	6 repeats with an 8″ or larger design repeat	6 repeats with an 8″ or larger design repeat	6 repeats with a 10″ or larger design repeat
Gold	¼ yard	⅜ yard	⅝ yard
Brown	⅓ yard	⅜ yard	⅝ yard
Blue	⅓ yard	½ yard	⅝ yard
Black	2½ yards	4⅛ yards	6⅓ yards
Border	⅝ yard	¾ yard	1¾ yards
Binding	½ yard	⅝ yard	⅞ yard
Backing	3¼ yards	4¾ yards	8¼ yards
Batting	59″ × 58″	75″ × 85″	98″ × 112″

Cutting

Refer to Triangle Block Basics (page 5) as needed. Use patterns A, B, C, D, Dr, G, and Gr (pages 72 and 73) to make templates. Refer to Special Cutting Techniques (page 46) for E, F, parallelograms, and trapezoids. Label each stack of cut pieces.

	WALL	THROW	QUEEN
Print*			
Template A	7 sets	13 sets	23 sets
Gold			
Template B	6	24	48
Template C	6	24	48
Brown			
Template B	18	24	48
Template C	18	24	48
Blue			
Template B	18	30	42
Template C	18	30	42

Cutting chart continued on next page

Cutting chart continued...

	WALL	THROW	QUEEN
Black			
Template D/Dr	42 pairs	78 pairs	138 pairs
8¼″ × WOF**	1 strip; subcut template G/Gr	1 strip; subcut template G/Gr	2 strips; subcut template G/Gr
Template G/Gr	4 pairs	4 pairs	8 pairs
8¼″ × WOF**	3 strips; subcut the following shapes:	7 strips; subcut the following shapes:	13 strips; subcut the following shapes:
E shape 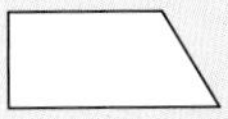	2 at 13¾″ long	2 at 4¾″ long	2 at 13¾″ long
F shape 	2 at 13¾″ long	2 at 4¾″ long 2 at 13¾″ long 2 at 27¼″ long	2 at 13¾″ long
Left parallelogram 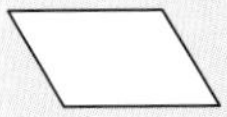	-	2 at 9″ long	
Right parallelogram 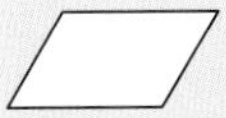	-		4 at 27″ long
Trapezoid 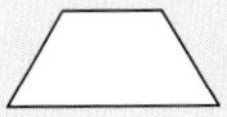	-	2 at 9″ long 2 at 18″ long	12 at 9″ long
Border			
2¾″ × WOF**	6 strips	8 strips	5 strips
6½″ × WOF**	-	-	6 strips
Binding			
2¼″ × WOF**	6 strips	8 strips	11 strips

* From the print fabric, cut 6 strips the width of the design repeat. Stack the 6 strips as described in Layered Cutting (page 46). Pin together each set of 6 strips, and then cut using Template A.

** WOF = width of fabric

Make the Triangle Blocks

All seam allowances are ¼″. Refer to Making the Triangle Block (page 7) as needed.

Make the following triangle blocks as shown.

	GOLD	BLUE	BROWN
WALL	6 (1 set of 6 matching A pieces)	18 (3 sets of 6 matching A pieces)	18 (3 sets of 6 matching A pieces)
THROW	24 (4 sets of 6 matching A pieces)	30 (5 sets of 6 matching A pieces)	24 (4 sets of 6 matching A pieces)
QUEEN	48 (8 sets of 6 matching A pieces)	42 (7 sets of 6 matching A pieces)	48 (8 sets of 6 matching A pieces)

Assemble the Quilt

1. Arrange the triangle blocks and background pieces as shown in the quilt assembly diagrams. Use a matching set of triangles blocks to form each star.

2. Sew the triangles into vertical columns. Press the seams open.

3. Sew the columns together. Press seams open.

4. Refer to Borders (page 76) to add the 2¾″ borders to the wall and throw size. For the queen size, use the 6½″ strips for the side border and the 2¾″ strips for the top and bottom border.

Quilt assembly—wall size 51″ × 50″

Quilt assembly—throw size 67″ × 77″

Quilt assembly—queen size 90″ × 104″

Finish the Quilt

Refer to Quiltmaking Basics (page 75) to layer, quilt, and bind the quilt. Quilt as desired. Use the 2¼″ binding strips to finish the quilt.

Detail of quilting: Additional stars are created with quilted outline filled with pebbles. Sets of three lines run diagonally across quilt.

Color Options

The white background, the blue outline, and the red stars create a patriotic theme.

The variation in the star outlines creates movement among the stars on this sea-green background.

The contrast of the light yellow and the dark red sets the stars apart in this arrangement.

The gold background and dark red outline of the stars provide a bold contrast.

Layered Cutting

This technique is a quick and easy way to create a design within the Template A shape by taking advantage of the design on the fabric. Unlike fussy cutting—in which you place a template on one design motif, cut, then move to the next identical motif, and so on—this technique allows you to cut multiple identical pieces at once by aligning the printed motif on several layers of fabric and cutting strips through all the layers. You can then cut identical pieces from the strips. This stacking method saves both fabric and time.

Following are steps for creating six identical shapes from layers of fabric. This method is based on finding the design repeats where the size of the repeat is the distance along the selvage from the start of a design motif to the point where that motif appears again.

1. Cut 1 strip of fabric that is the width of the repeat × half the width of the fabric. This piece will be your guide for cutting the next pieces. Cut the number of strips needed for the size quilt you are making (see Cutting, page 42).

2. Stack and align the layers. Choose a motif you want to feature in the triangle. Carefully place a pin vertically through all the layers at the same spot, so the same motif is lined up in each layer. Repeat across the strip length. Place pin through same spot on each layer.

Place pin through same spot on each layer.

3. Insert another pin through all the layers as shown. Then remove the first pin; the second pin will keep the layers from shifting.

Second pin keeps fabrics from shifting.

4. Use a ruler and rotary cutter to cut a strip through all the layers the width given in the cutting instruction. Now you're ready to subcut the strip into specific shapes, such as the Template A shape. As you cut each stack into pieces, pin those pieces together so you can use the pieces from the same stack all in the same star when you are ready to arrange the star in the quilt.

Stack of shapes for desired pattern

Cutting Special Shapes: Parallelograms, E, F, and Trapezoids

Use the G/Gr pattern (page 73) to make a G/Gr template, referring to Making Plastic Templates for the Projects (page 6). Then trim the template on the ¼″ seamline marked on the left side of the template as shown. (Do not trim the seam allowances on the other sides of the template.) Rename this template "special G/Gr," and use it only to cut the parallelograms, the trapezoids, the E shapes, and the F shapes in this project.

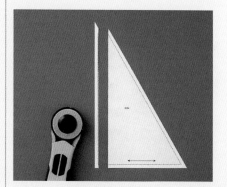

Trim off template seam allowance as shown.

Cutting Left and Right Parallelogram Shapes

To cut a left parallelogram:

1. Cut a strip 8¼″ × width of fabric.

2. With fabric facing up, place the special G/Gr template on the fabric strip as shown. Align a ruler with the right edge of the template and cut with a rotary cutter. Then use a removable marker to draw a line along the left edge of the template.

Cut on right template edge and draw line on left template edge.

3. Refer to Cutting (pages 42 and 43) for the desired parallelogram length. From the line marked on the fabric, measure the indicated length to the left and draw another line on the fabric. This example measures 9¼″ from line to line.

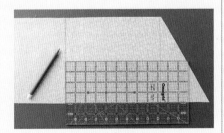

Line to line is 9¼″.

4. With the template positioned as shown, align the right edge of template on the new line and cut along the left edge of the template. You have cut a left parallelogram.

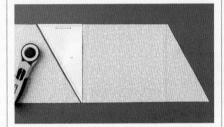

Cut on left edge of template.

To cut a right parallelogram:

Flip the special G template and repeat Steps 1–4 of the instructions above.

Cutting Trapezoid Shapes

1. Repeat Steps 1 and 2 of Cutting Parallelogram Shapes (page 47).

2. Refer to Cutting (pages 42 and 43) for the desired trapezoid length. From the line marked on the fabric, measure the indicated length and draw another line on the fabric. This example measures 9¼″ from line to line.

Line to line is 9¼″.

3. With the template positioned as shown, align the right edge of template on the new line and cut along the left edge of the template. You have cut a unique trapezoid.

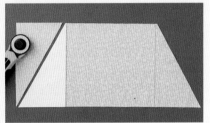

Cut on left side of template.

Cutting E Shapes

1. Repeat Steps 1–3 of Cutting Parallelogram Shapes (page 47).

2. Refer to Cutting (pages 42 and 43) for the desired E length. From the line marked on the fabric, measure the indicated length and draw another line on the fabric. This example measures 9¼″ from line to line.

Line to line is 9¼″.

3. Cut on the newly drawn line.

Special Cutting Techniques continued...

Cutting F Shapes

1. Cut a strip 8¼˝ × width of fabric.

2. With fabric facing up, place the special G/Gr template on the fabric strip as shown. Align a ruler with the right edge of the template and cut with a rotary cutter. Then use a removable marker to draw a line along the left edge of the template.

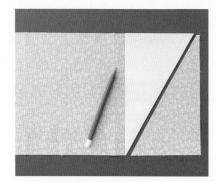

Cut on right edge of template and mark left template edge.

3. Refer to Cutting (pages 42 and 43) for the desired F length. From the line marked on the fabric, measure the indicated length and draw another line on the fabric. This example measures 9¼˝ from line to line.

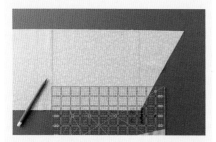

Line to line is 9¼˝.

4. Cut on the newly drawn line.

Starry Lights

FINISHED SIZE: 39″ × 41″ (wall size)

Project Lesson:
Use Negative Space to Create Shapes

The negative space is the area around the star and not the star itself. Ideally negative space forms an interesting and artistically relevant shape, making the background the focus rather than the stars. This quilt is created by outlining the stars in a similar color but darker value. Ten different red fabrics of roughly the same value are used randomly for the background shield shape.

Materials

	WALL 39″ × 54″	TWIN 70″ × 90″	QUEEN 90″ × 111″
Red (10 red fabrics that are roughly the same value)	½ yard each of 10 reds	¾ yard each of 10 reds	¾ yard each of 10 reds
Cream	1 yard	2½ yards	2⅞ yards
Gold	⅞ yard	2⅜ yards	2⅞ yards
Border	-	-	2⅛ yards
Binding	½ yard	¾ yard	⅞ yard
Backing	2⅝ yards	5½ yards	8¼ yards
Batting	47″ × 62″	78″ × 90″	98″ × 119″

Cutting

Refer to Triangle Block Basics (page 5) as needed to make templates and cut strips. Use patterns A, B, C, D, and Dr (pages 72 and 73). Label each stack of cut pieces.

	WALL	THROW	QUEEN
10 shades of red			
Template D/Dr	60 pairs (6 pairs from each fabric)	190 pairs (19 pairs from each fabric)	230 pairs (23 pairs from each fabric)
Cream			
Template A	55	189	230
Gold			
Template B	55	189	230
Template C	55	189	230
Border (6½″ × WOF*)	-	-	10 strips
Binding (2¼″ × WOF*)	5 strips	9 strips	11 strips

* WOF = width of fabric

Make the Triangle Blocks

All seam allowances are ¼″. Refer to Making the Triangle Block (page 7) as needed.

Sew a gold B and a gold C piece to all the cream A pieces. Press the seams toward the cream. To complete each triangle block, randomly add a D and a Dr, and press the seams toward the red. For the wall-size quilt make 55 triangle blocks. For the twin-size quilt, make 189 triangle blocks. For the queen-size quilt, make 230 triangle blocks. (You will have extra D/Dr pieces left from the wall- and twin-size quilts.)

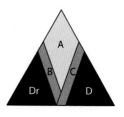

Assemble the Quilt

1. Arrange the triangle blocks as shown in the quilt assembly diagrams.

2. Sew the blocks into vertical columns. Press the seams open.

3. Sew the columns together. Press the seams open.

4. Trim off the triangle units as needed.

5. Refer to Borders (page 76) to add the 6½″ border to the queen-size quilt.

Quilt assembly—wall size 39″ × 54″

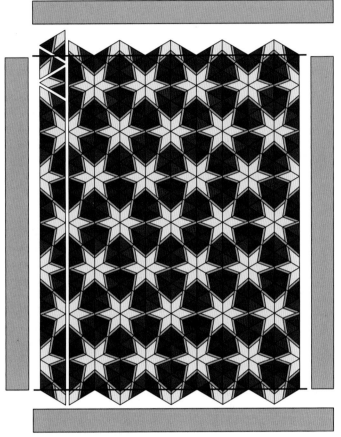

Quilt assembly—queen size 90″ × 111″

Quilt assembly—twin size 70″ × 90″

Finish the Quilt

Refer to Quiltmaking Basics (page 75) to layer, quilt, and bind the quilt. Quilt as desired. Use the 2¼″ binding strips to finish the quilt.

Detail of quilting: Insides of stars are echo-quilted three times, and inside the center a star is quilted with small circles.

Color Options

In this color option, the negative space is created by yellow hexagons, and then black is used for the stars with a gray outline.

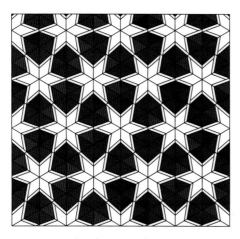

The negative space has horizontal zigzag bands in shades of red across the background. The light outlines of the stars create large stars to contrast with the background.

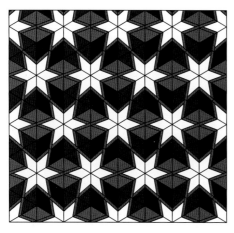

Horizontal bands of light and dark purple are created with the careful placement of the purple shades in the negative space. With the purple outlines around these stars, the stars appear smaller than in the previous example.

Life Lesson: The Fellowship of Quilting

Quilting and sewing are not my passions; you will never hear the words *expert* or *talented* in the same sentence as *quilting* and *sewing* and my name. I quilt because I have learned that quilting is more than a job or hobby; quilting for me is a heritage and time of fellowship.

My mother's family is made up of generations of talented quilters and seamstresses, but at the roots of sewing within the family was a need to sew. The ladies of the family needed to clothe their loved ones and keep them warm during cold winter nights with their quilted handiwork; sewing was a way of life.

For most people in today's world quilting and sewing are something done for pleasure. However, for me the pleasure is not in the piecing of a quilt, the humming of the machine, or the reveal of the finished product. I gain pleasure from sitting down with my sisters for an afternoon of sewing and coffee, seeking the wisdom of my mother and aunts when I am not certain of my next step, and watching my grandmother continue working at her craft in her elder years. I have learned to enjoy sewing for the skill set it is, but that is not the driving passion to place me in front of a sewing machine.

My daughters are not only being exposed to a fading skill set, but they are also learning to enjoy moments together as family and to seek the wisdom of their elders. I am not certain if my daughters will embrace quilting or sewing as a hobby, but I do hope that they learn to embrace a better understanding of their heritage and the fellowship that can happen when a group of quilters get together. The lessons I have learned from sewing in fellowship did not simply improve my sewing skills. I have learned how to love my husband, teach my children, enjoy my current phase in life, for it won't last long, and most importantly, I have learned that family is woven together through fellowship and love.

—Jillian Crawford

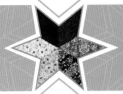

Cubes-Cubes

FINISHED SIZE: 62″ × 72″ (throw size)

PROJECT LESSON:
Use Overlays and Fabric Values to Create Depth

An overlay is tulle, nylon netting, organdy, or any sheer fabric that you place over another fabric to create a darker or lighter value. It is an easy way to change the value of fabric you already have. Place the desired overlay over the piece of fabric and stitch it into the seam.

Each of the cubes in this quilt is created with one fabric. The three values are created by using three colors of tulle as overlays: black, smoke, and white. White and smoke tulle overlays are used on the black print fabrics and black tulle is used on the white background fabrics.

Look at a white cube and you will see that its top diamonds are the lightest value (no tulle), the left diamonds are the darkest value (two layers of tulle), and the right diamonds are the middle value of the cube (one layer of tulle).

If there were no tulle overlays on the quilt and the triangle blocks were rotated, the cubes would disappear and you would see stars centered on the hexagons.

《alert》

An iron on the cotton setting can melt tulle, nylon netting, organdy, and many other sheer fabrics. Use a synthetic setting when pressing the overlays, or use a pressing cloth.

《tip》

To get a light value, choose fabric with a white background and a fine black pattern. For dark values, look for fabrics with a black background and a fine white pattern. None of the fabrics in this quilt are gray.

With no overlay, one would see hexagons.

I recommend this technique just for smaller quilts—the overlays are fragile and need to be hand washed. If you want to make a larger bed-sized quilt, you can achieve the same effect by using three different fabrics in each cube instead of overlays.

Materials

Choose shades of black print fabrics in light, medium, and dark values.

	WALL 31″ × 45″	THROW 62″ × 72″	DOUBLE 78″ × 99″
Black prints	½ yard each of 6 prints	⅝ yard each of 10 prints	1 yard each of 10 prints
Vibrant blue	½ yard	1½ yards	2¾ yards
White tulle 90″ wide	¼ yard	½ yard	¾ yard
Smoke tulle 90″ wide	¼ yard	½ yard	¾ yard
Black tulle 90″ wide	¼ yard	½ yard	¾ yard
Binding	½ yard	⅝ yard	⅞ yard
Backing	2½ yards	3¾ yards	7¼ yards
Batting	39″ × 57″	70″ × 80″	86″ × 107″

Cutting

Refer to Triangle Block Basics (page 5) as needed to make templates and cut strips.

Use patterns A, B, C, D, and Dr (pages 72 and 73). Label each stack of cut pieces.

	WALL	THROW	DOUBLE
Black prints			
Template A	6 from each print	12 from each print	21 from each print
Template D/Dr	6 pairs from each print	12 pairs from each print	21 pairs from each print
Vibrant blue			
Template B	36	120	210
Template C	36	120	210
Binding (2¼″ × WOF*)	5 strips	7 strips	11 strips
White tulle 4¾″ × 6½″	36 pieces	120 pieces	210 pieces
Smoke tulle 4¾″ × 6½″	36 pieces	120 pieces	210 pieces
Black tulle 4¾″ × 6½″	36 pieces	120 pieces	210 pieces

* WOF = width of fabric

Note: More tulle pieces are cut than needed—the number needed will depend on what color of tulle looks best with the fabrics.

Make the Cubes

All seam allowances are ¼″. Refer to Making the Triangle Block (page 7) as needed.

For this quilt, tulle is placed on top of pieces A, D, and Dr, and does not cover the vibrant blue strips. For each block, determine which color of tulle and how many layers are needed to get the values you want.

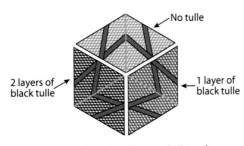

Layers of black tulle on a light cube 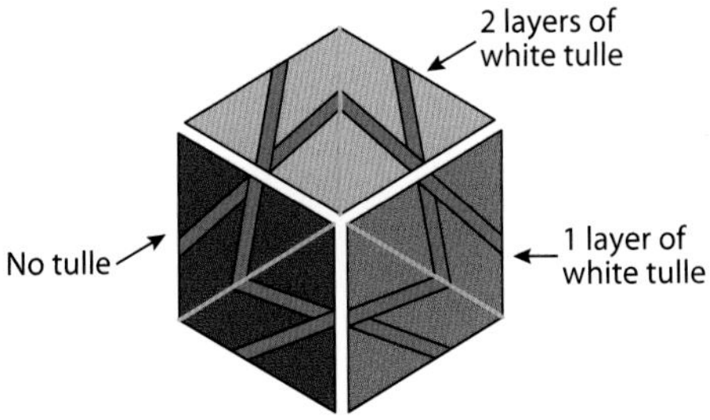   Layers of white tulle on a black cube

Each cube requires 6 triangle blocks, and a half-cube has 3 triangle blocks. The wall quilt has 5 cubes and 2 half-cubes. The twin size has 18 cubes and 4 half-cubes. The double size has 32 cubes and 6 half-cubes. For each cube or half-cube, follow these steps:

1. Use the block diagrams in the quilt assembly diagrams (pages 56 and 57) to plan the fabric placement for your project.

2. Place tulle over A pieces as needed. Sew vibrant blue B and C pieces onto the A pieces.

3. Place tulle over D and Dr pieces as needed.

4. Sew each triangle block together. *Note: Cubes will not be sewn together until all the blocks are made and arranged on a design wall.*

5. Repeat Steps 1–4 for each color of cube and half-cube.

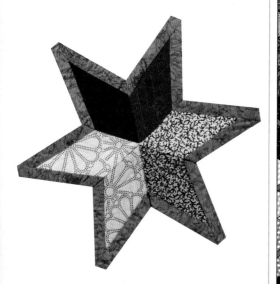

Assemble the Quilt

1. Arrange the triangle blocks on a design wall as shown in the quilt assembly diagrams (pages 56 and 57).

2. Sew the triangles into vertical columns. Press the seams open.

3. Sew the columns together. Press the seams open.

4. The points at the top and bottom of the quilt maintain the cube effect in the finished quilt, so do not trim the top and bottom of the quilt top.

Quilt assembly—wall size 31˝ × 45˝

Quilt assembly—throw size 62˝ × 72˝

Quilt assembly—double size 78″ × 99″

Finish the Quilt

Refer to Quiltmaking Basics (page 75) to layer, quilt, and bind the quilt. Quilt as desired. Use the 2¼″ binding strips to finish the quilt.

Detail of quilting: Straight lines help define each cube.

Color Options

A cube can also be created by using three different fabrics instead of overlays.

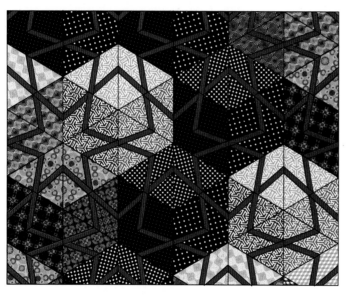

Here's a more subtle use of three different fabrics to create cubes.

Life Lesson: Every Piece Counts

I've come to realize that my favorite quilts are scrappy. You know the ones—those made with a myriad of fabrics and colors. The greater the variety of fabrics, the better the effect. When the whole luscious quilt is admired, the mixture of fabrics creates a perfect quilt design with a balance of contrasting lights and darks, and the magnificent blend of colors melts into a thing of beauty. Close inspection of each fabric, though, reveals that some of the quilt pieces are absolutely gorgeous while other pieces are not at all beautiful. In fact, some of the fabric pieces may be downright ugly, but in a scrappy quilt each fabric piece fills an important role in making the whole quilt beautiful.

I think that's the way it is with life. I've had so many, many good and lovely experiences in my life, and yet I've also had sad, unhappy calamities that I wouldn't choose. Along the way I've learned and grown through the tough times and the good times. All my life experiences merge together to make me, and I have a very scrappy and happy, beautiful life! I am so blessed.

—Susan Nelsen

Interlocking Cubes and Stars

Surprise Packages

FINISHED SIZE: 62″ × 77″ (throw size)

Project Lesson:
Make Large and Small Cubes with Shadows

In this quilt, the large cube is made by coloring the background of eight triangle blocks with a dark-value fabric, eight triangle blocks with a medium-value fabric, and eight triangle blocks with a light-value fabric. Each group of triangle blocks makes one side of the cube. A colored star is created on each side of the large cube. Note: Wall size does not include the big cube.

Each of the small cubes is made by coloring two triangle blocks with a dark value, two triangle blocks with a medium value, and two triangle blocks with a light value. Two legs of the interlocking stars are colored using the same color as the cube, but the outline of the star is a different color.

Shadows of the cubes are created by using a dark shade of fabric on the right bottom side of the cube.

To create this marvelous effect, pick nine fabrics for the cubes: three teals, three yellows, and three purples. Each color groups needs a dark, medium, and light value so there is enough contrast between each fabric to see each side of the cube. The background will be a light and a dark gray to create the shadow effect.

Materials

	WALL 31″ × 59″	THROW 62″ × 77″	QUEEN 98″ × 106″
3 shades of teal	½ yard each	⅞ yard each	1 yard each
3 shades of yellow	½ yard each	⅞ yard each	1 yard each
3 shades of purple	½ yard each	1 yard each	1 yard each
Light gray	1 yard	2⅛ yards	4¾ yards
Dark gray	⅝ yard	⅞ yard	⅞ yard
Accent border	-	-	1⅝ yards
Border	-	-	2⅜ yards
Binding	½ yard	⅝ yard	⅞ yard
Backing	2 yards	4¾ yards	8⅞ yards
Batting	39″ × 67″	70″ × 85″	106″ × 114″

Cutting

Refer to Triangle Block Basics (page 5) as needed to make templates and cut strips. Use patterns A, B, C, D, and Dr (pages 72 and 73). Label each stack of cut pieces.

	WALL	THROW	QUEEN
Light teal			
Template A	2	4	4
Template B	6	15	23
Template C	6	15	23
Template D/Dr	2 pairs	10 pairs	10 pairs
Medium teal			
Template A	2	4	4
Template B	6	15	23
Template C	6	15	23
Template D/Dr	2 pairs	10 pairs	10 pairs
Dark teal			
Template A	2	4	4
Template B	6	15	23
Template C	6	15	23
Template D/Dr	2 pairs	10 pairs	10 pairs
Light yellow			
Template A	2	4	4
Template B	6	15	23
Template C	6	15	23
Template D/Dr	2 pairs	4 pairs	4 pairs
Medium yellow			
Template A	2	4	4
Template B	6	15	23
Template C	6	15	23
Template D/Dr	2 pairs	4 pairs	4 pairs
Dark yellow			
Template A	2	4	4
Template B	6	15	23
Template C	6	15	23
Template D/Dr	2 pairs	4 pairs	4 pairs

	WALL	THROW	QUEEN
Light purple			
Template A	4	12	12
Template B	6	15	23
Template C	6	15	23
Template D/Dr	4 pairs	6 pairs	6 pairs
Medium purple			
Template A	4	12	12
Template B	6	15	23
Template C	6	15	23
Template D/Dr	4 pairs	6 pairs	6 pairs
Dark purple			
Template A	4	12	12
Template B	6	15	23
Template C	6	15	23
Template D/Dr	4 pairs	6 pairs	6 pairs
Light gray			
Template A	19	54	123
Template D/Dr	19 pairs	54 pairs	123 pairs
Dark gray			
Template A	5	14	17
Template D/Dr	5 pairs	14 pairs	17 pairs
Accent border			
1½″ × WOF*	-	-	33 strips
Border			
4″ × WOF*	-	-	19 strips
Binding			
2¼″ × WOF*	5 strips	8 strips	11 strips

* WOF = width of fabric

Make the Triangle Blocks

All seam allowances are ¼". Refer to Making the Triangle Block (page 7) as needed.

BIG CUBE

This big cube is only in the throw- and queen-size quilts, so you do not need to make any of these blocks for the wall-size quilt. If making the wall-size quilt, skip to Little Cubes (below).

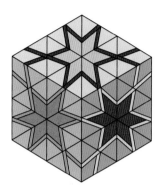

Make the following blocks as shown. Do not join these blocks together, but keep the cube sets together.

Make 6 of each triangle block.

Make 2 of each triangle block.

LITTLE CUBES

Read the instructions for each small cube, as not all of them are used in every size. Make the blocks, but do not join the blocks together.

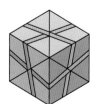

Teal cube for *all* sizes

For the little teal cube, make the following blocks as shown. Do not join these blocks together, but keep the cube sets together.

Make 2 of each triangle block for teal cube.

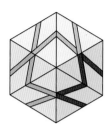

Yellow cube A for *all* sizes

For the little yellow cube A, make the following blocks as shown. Do not join these blocks together, but keep the cube sets together.

Make 2 of each triangle block for yellow cube A.

Purple cube A for *all* sizes

For the little purple cube A, make the following blocks as shown. Do not join these blocks together, but keep the cube sets together.

Make 2 of each triangle block for purple cube A.

Purple cube B for *all* sizes

For the little purple cube B, make the following blocks as shown. Do not join these blocks together, but keep the cube sets together.

Make 2 of each triangle block for purple cube B.

Yellow cube B only for throw and queen sizes

For the little yellow cube B, make the following blocks as shown. Do not join these blocks together, but keep the cube sets together.

Make 2 of each triangle block for yellow cube B.

Purple cube C only for throw and queen sizes

For little purple cube C, make the following blocks as shown. Do not join these blocks together, but keep the cube sets together.

Make 2 of each triangle block for purple cube C.

BACKGROUND TRIANGLES

Use light gray A and light gray D/Dr pieces, with 2 matching B and C pieces, to make each background triangle block. You can select the matching B and C pieces randomly. Make 19 for wall, 54 for throw, and 123 for queen size.

Make 19 (wall), 54 (throw), or 123 (queen) background triangle blocks.

SHADOW TRIANGLES

Use dark gray A and dark gray D/Dr pieces, with 2 matching B and C pieces, to make each shadow triangle block. You can select the matching B and C pieces randomly. Make 5 for wall, 14 for throw, and 17 for queen size. When you are finished, you will have extra B and C pieces remaining.

Make 5 (wall), 14 (throw), or 17 (queen) shadow triangles blocks.

Assemble the Quilt

Refer to the quilt assembly diagrams (pages 64 and 65).

1. For the throw and queen sizes, arrange the big teal cube first. For the wall size, arrange the small teal cube first.

2. Add shadow triangles to the big teal cube or the small teal cube. Add the background triangles according to the quilt assembly diagrams.

3. Add the purple cube and shadows.

4. Continuing to look at the quilt assembly diagram, add background gray triangle blocks and the rest of the cubes and shadows.

5. Sew the triangle blocks together in vertical columns, pressing the seams open.

6. Sew together the columns. Press the seams open.

7. After the columns are joined and pressed, trim the columns as shown in the diagrams.

8. Refer to Borders (page 76) to add the borders to the queen-size quilt, using the accent border 1½˝ strips and the border 4˝ strips.

Quilt assembly—wall size 31˝ × 59˝

Quilt assembly—throw size 62˝ × 77˝

Quilt assembly—queen size 98″ × 106″

Finish the Quilt

Refer to Quiltmaking Basics (page 75) to layer, quilt, and bind the quilt. Quilt as desired. Use the 2¼″ binding strips to finish the quilt.

Color Options

Detail of quilting: Notice different quilting patterns in different portions of quilt.

White background

Black background with no shadow effect

Autumnal orange, green, and tan

Life Lesson:
Learning from Grandmother

I remember spending time during the summers when I was in elementary school at my grandparents' farm. My grandmother stayed busy from dawn to late evenings. She had raised nine children who were all grown and away from home. A lot of her time was spent with activities to raise money for her church and for missions. There was no idle time spent sitting around. She would crochet beautiful doilies, bedspreads, tablecloths, and other items for sale.

She also made her own clothing (as she had for her children). The odd small pieces we were allowed to use to practice our hand sewing. Pieces of any size were cut in strips, sewn together, wound in balls, and used to make "rag" rugs. Making these strips was my first experience using a sewing machine (treadle of course). Even though I was cautioned to go slowly, I was sure I could get the strips made quickly—resulting in having the machine needle through my finger. I didn't hear an "I told you." I think she thought I had learned my lesson. I had! Those rugs were used in her house and those of her children. Any left were sold.

My grandparents worked hard their entire lives. But work was done from early Monday morning until late Saturday evening—cows to be milked, chickens to be fed, gardens to be tended, and much more. Sunday was for church and rest. If you visited on Saturday, you might get to lick the spice cake mixing bowl or peel bananas for between the layers and on top. We also might get to churn butter to put on homemade bread. Sunday's lunch was prepared on Saturday. So we knew what we had to look forward to when we went to Grandma's house on Sunday.

I enjoy sewing and piecing quilts. I am involved with a group of women from our church who crochet prayer shawls that are donated to the local cancer center. I think seeing my grandmother take time from her work to help others and find ways to make the world a better place was definitely an influence on my life.

All these things seem so long ago now. We are so busy being busy that we don't seem to have time for family visits, spice cake made from scratch, relaxing as you hand stitch the border on a quilt that is almost complete. My grandmother may have "gone to town" once a month, but she had everything she needed and a family that loved her. Maybe we need to slow down and smell Grandma's flowers, do our handwork, and use the skills God has given us to make the world a better place, as my grandmother did, six days a week, and rest on the seventh.

—Joyce Davis

other design IDEAS

What you've seen in this book are just a few of the possibilities using the basic triangle block I've described in Triangle Block Basics (page 7). But there are so many more quilts that can be designed, just by changing colors and values!

Here are a few additional designs I've created, and a line drawing of the grid (page 69) I use to design. You can use the grid to design your own quilts. Use the cutting chart (page 7), and you're on your way to making any triangle block quilt you like.

AMAZINGLY SIMPLE TRIANGLE STARS

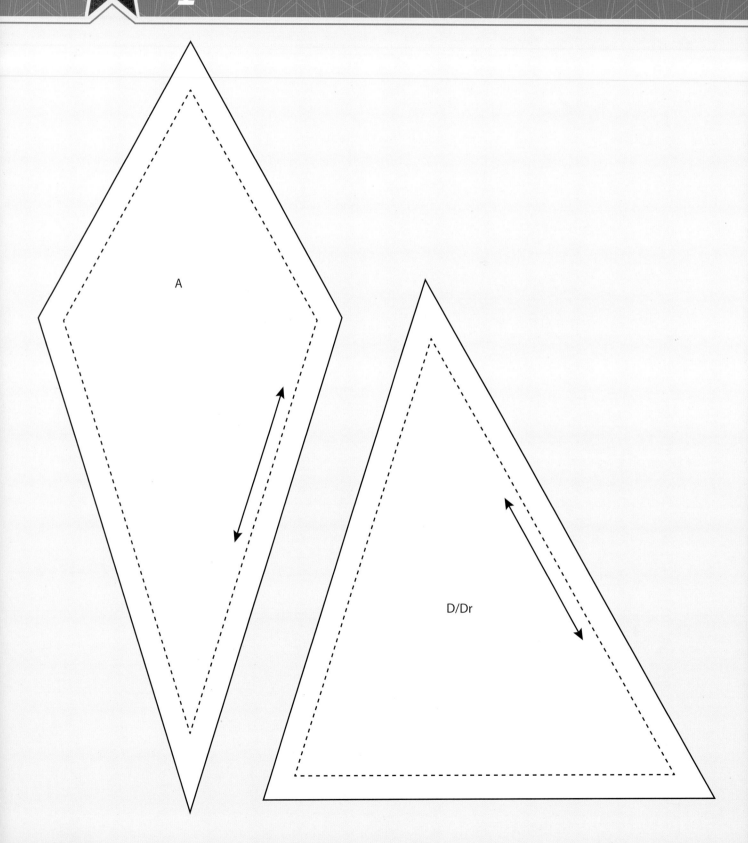

A

D/Dr

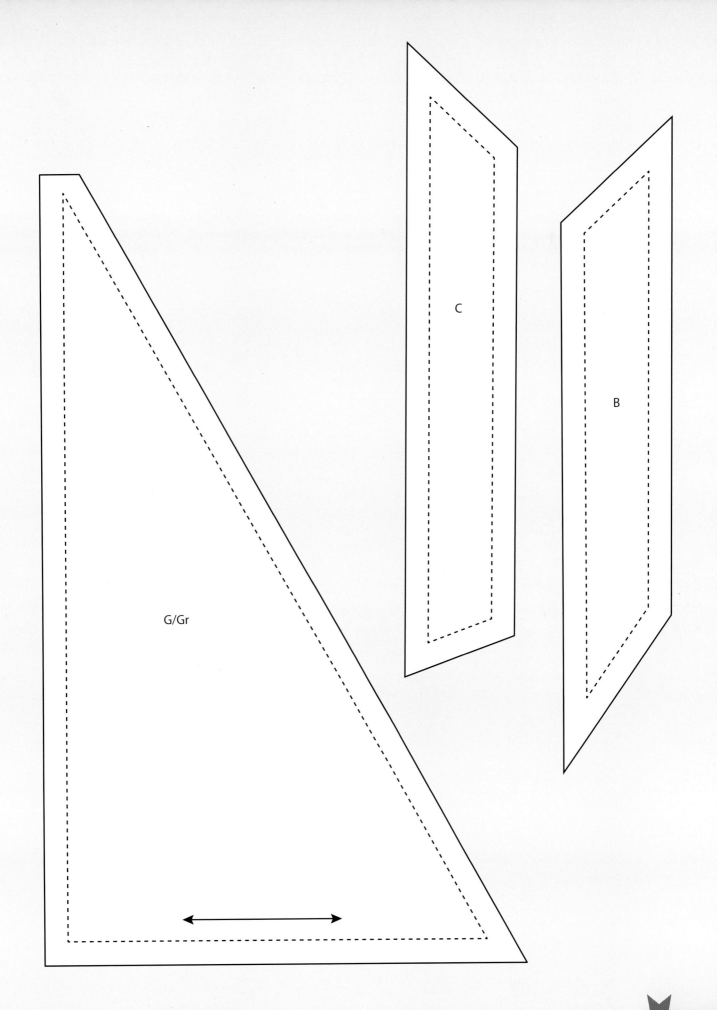

C

B

G/Gr

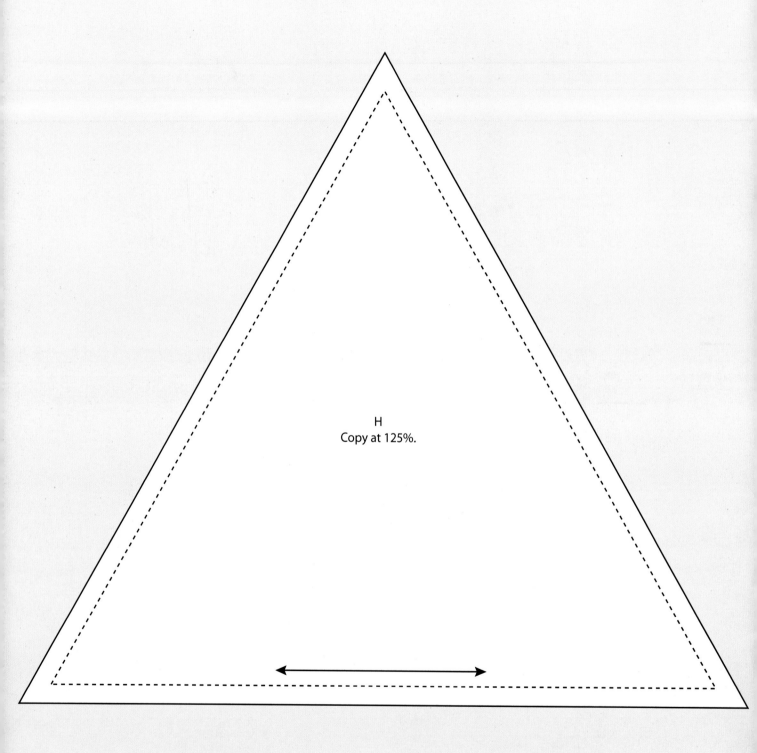

H
Copy at 125%.

quiltmaking
B A S I C S

General Guidelines

SEAM ALLOWANCES

A ¼″ seam allowance is used for most projects. It's a good idea to do a test seam before you begin sewing to check that your ¼″ is accurate. Accuracy is the key to successful piecing.

There is no need to backstitch. Seamlines will be crossed by another seam, which will anchor them.

PRESSING

In general, press seams toward the darker fabric. Press lightly in an up-and-down motion. Avoid using a very hot iron or over-ironing, which can distort shapes and blocks. Be especially careful when pressing bias edges, as they stretch easily.

Borders

When border strips are cut on the crosswise grain, piece the strips together to achieve the needed lengths.

In most cases the side borders are sewn on first. When you have finished the quilt top, measure it through the center vertically. This will be the length to cut the side borders. Place pins at the centers of all four sides of the quilt top, as well as in the center of each side border strip. Pin the side borders to the quilt top first, matching the center pins. Using a ¼″ seam allowance, sew the borders to the quilt top and press toward the border.

Measure horizontally across the center of the quilt top including the side borders. This will be the length to cut the top and bottom borders. Repeat, pinning, sewing, and pressing.

Backing

Plan on making the backing a minimum of 8″ longer and wider than the quilt top. Piece, if necessary. Trim the selvages before you piece to the desired size.

To economize, piece the back from any leftover quilting fabrics or blocks in your collection.

Batting

The type of batting to use is a personal decision; consult your local quilt shop. Cut batting approximately 8″ longer and wider than your quilt top. Note that your batting choice will affect how much quilting is necessary for the quilt. Check the manufacturer's instructions to see how far apart the quilting lines can be.

Layering

Spread the backing wrong side up and tape the edges down with masking tape. (If you are working on carpet you can use T-pins to secure the backing to the carpet.) Center the batting on top, smoothing out any folds. Place the quilt top right side up on top of the batting and backing, making sure it is centered.

Basting

Basting keeps the quilt "sandwich" layers from shifting while you are quilting.

If you plan to machine quilt on your domestic machine, pin baste the quilt layers together with safety pins placed about 3″–4″ apart. Begin basting in the center and move toward the edges first in vertical, then horizontal, rows. Try not to pin directly on the intended quilting lines.

If you plan to hand quilt, baste the layers together with thread using a long needle and light-colored thread. Knot one end of the thread. Using stitches approximately the length of the needle, begin in the center and move out toward the edges in vertical and horizontal rows approximately 4″ apart. Add 2 diagonal rows of basting.

Quilting

Quilting, whether by hand or machine, enhances the pieced or appliquéd design of the quilt. You may choose to quilt in-the-ditch, echo the pieced or appliquéd motifs, use patterns from quilting design books and stencils, or do your own free-motion quilting. Remember to check the batting manufacturer's recommendations for how close the quilting lines must be.

Binding

After the quilting is complete, trim excess batting and backing from the quilt even with the edges of the quilt top.

DOUBLE-FOLD STRAIGHT-GRAIN BINDING

If you want a ¼″ finished binding, cut the binding strips 2¼″ wide and piece them together with diagonal seams to make a continuous binding strip. Trim the seam allowance to ¼″. Press the seams open.

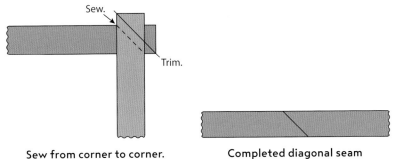

Sew from corner to corner.   Completed diagonal seam

Press the entire strip in half lengthwise with wrong sides together. With raw edges even, pin the binding to the front edge of the quilt a few inches away from a corner, and leave the first few inches of the binding unattached. Start sewing, using a ¼″ seam allowance.

Stop ¼″ away from the first corner (Step 1), and backstitch one stitch. Lift the presser foot and needle. Rotate the quilt one-quarter turn. Fold the binding at a right angle so it extends straight above the quilt and the fold forms a 45° angle in the corner (Step 2). Then bring the binding strip down even with the edge of the quilt (Step 3). Begin sewing at the folded edge. Repeat in the same manner at all corners.

CONTINUOUS BIAS BINDING

A continuous bias involves using a square sliced in half diagonally and then sewing the triangles together so that you continuously cut marked strips to make continuous bias binding. The same instructions can be used to cut bias for piping. Cut the fabric for the bias binding or piping so it is a square. For example, if yardage is ½ yard, cut an 18″ × 18″ square. Cut the square in half diagonally, creating 2 triangles.

Sew these triangles together as shown, using a ¼″ seam allowance. Press the seam open.

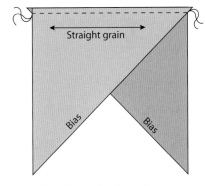

Sew triangles together.

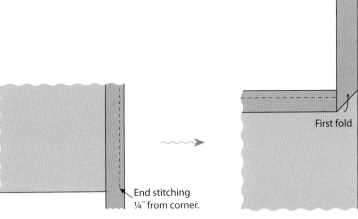

STEP 1. Stitch to ⅓″ from corner.   STEP 2. First fold for miter

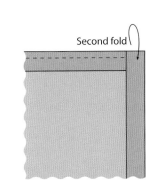

STEP 3. Second fold alignment

Continue stitching until you are back near the beginning of the binding strip. See Finishing the Binding Ends (page 78) for tips on finishing and hiding the raw edges of the ends of the binding.

Using a ruler, mark the parallelogram created by the 2 triangles with lines spaced the width you need to cut the bias strip. Cut about 5″ along the first line.

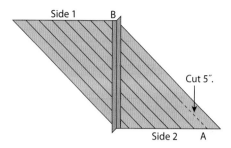

Mark lines and begin cut.

Join Side 1 and Side 2 to form a tube. The raw edge at point A will align with the raw edge at B. This will allow the first line to be offset by one strip width. Pin the raw edges right sides together, making sure that the drawn lines match. Sew with a ¼″ seam allowance. Press the seam open. Cut along the drawn lines, creating one continuous strip.

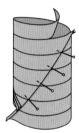

Press the entire strip in half lengthwise with wrong sides together. Place binding on quilt as described in Double-Fold Straight-Grain Binding (above).

See Finishing the Binding Ends (below) for tips on finishing and hiding the raw edges of the ends of the binding.

FINISHING THE BINDING ENDS

Method 1

After stitching around the quilt, fold under the beginning tail of the binding strip ¼″ so that the raw edge will be inside the binding after it is turned to the back of the quilt. Place the end tail of the binding strip over the beginning folded end. Continue to attach the binding and stitch slightly beyond the starting stitches. Trim the excess binding. Fold the binding over the raw edges to the quilt back and hand stitch, mitering the corners.

Method 2

See the tip at ctpub.com/quilting-sewing-tips > Completing a Binding with an Invisible Seam.

Fold the ending tail of the binding back on itself where it meets the beginning binding tail. From the fold, measure and mark the cut width of the binding strip. Cut the ending binding tail to this measurement. For example, if the binding is cut 2¼″ wide, measure from the fold on the ending tail of the binding 2¼″ and cut the binding tail to this length.

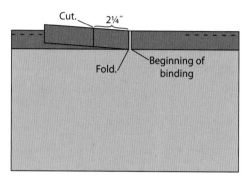

Cut binding tail.

Open both tails. Place one tail on top of the other tail at right angles, right sides together. Mark a diagonal line from corner to corner and stitch on the line. Check that you've done it correctly and that the binding fits the quilt; then trim the seam allowance to ¼″. Press open.

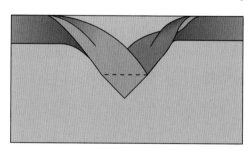

Stitch ends of binding diagonally.

Refold the binding and stitch this binding section in place on the quilt. Fold the binding over the raw edges to the quilt back and hand stitch.

About the Author

Barbara H. Cline started creating quilts in her teens. Since then, she has had more than 31 years of experience teaching quiltmaking classes at local sewing shops and creating beautiful quilts and patterns. Barbara worked at The Clothes Line fabric shop (now called Patchwork Plus) in Virginia from fifth grade until she married and had children. She became a stay-at-home mother who pieced quilt tops to sell when she had time. When her youngest child entered kindergarten, she started working part-time at The Clothes Line again.

Barbara currently teaches classes at Patchwork Plus & Sew Classics and loves to design and piece wallhangings and quilts from her home in Shenandoah Valley, Virginia. Her quilts have been shown and have won ribbons in various quilt shows and contests.

Barbara comes from a close-knit Mennonite family of quilters; her grandmother Vera Heatwole taught her daughters, granddaughters, great-granddaughters, great-great-granddaughters, and daughters-in-law to quilt. Every year the women gather for a sewing retreat, where they quilt, sew, and follow other creative pursuits. The family members and their quilts were featured in the Virginia Quilt Museum's exhibition *Five Generations of Mennonite Quilts*.

 Also by Barbara H. Cline:

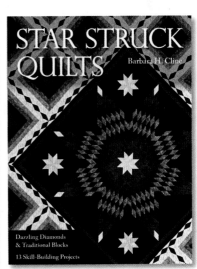